T0015714

REPTILE
PREDATORS

BY MIGNONNE GUNASEKARA

BookLife
PUBLISHING

©2022
BookLife Publishing Ltd.
King's Lynn
Norfolk PE30 4LS

ISBN: 978-1-80155-138-0

Written by:
Mignonne Gunasekara

Edited by:
Shalini Vallepur

Designed by:
Gareth Liddington

A catalogue record for this book is available from the British Library.

CONTENTS

MEET THE PREDATORS

Welcome to the world of predators. Predators are animals that hunt other animals for food. They come in many shapes and sizes, but they all have something in common – to the prey that they hunt, they are terrifying!

In this book, we will be looking at predators that are reptiles. Reptiles are scaly, cold-blooded animals that usually have a backbone. Cold-blooded animals have blood that changes temperature with the temperature around them.

GILA MONSTER

Gila monsters live in the desert. They are venomous, which means they can poison other animals by biting them. They sometimes chew while biting an animal to get their venom deep into the bite and into the animal's blood. They also steal eggs from other animals' nests to eat.

A Gila monster stores fat in its tail and body. This can keep it going when it has not eaten in a long time. This is useful because Gila monsters spend most of their lives underground where there might not be a lot of food.

ALLIGATOR SNAPPING TURTLE

Alligator snapping turtles are some of the largest turtles in the world. They live in rivers and lakes in the US and spend most of their lives in water. They hunt for fish and frogs using a lure that looks like a worm.

LURE

An alligator snapping turtle sits still and wiggles the red lure on its tongue. When prey gets close to have a look, the turtle snaps its mouth shut and eats the prey.

KING COBRA

The king cobra is the longest venomous snake in the world. It lives in forests in South Asia and Southeast Asia. It can climb trees and swim. Its main prey is other snakes, but the venom from one bite is enough to kill an elephant.

When king cobras are scared, they spread out their hoods. They also lift the front part of their bodies off the ground and keep moving forward to scare away animals that are scaring them.

CENTRAL BEARDED
DRAGON

Bearded dragons come from Australia, where they live in warm, dry habitats. A central bearded dragon's beard is made up of spiky scales around its chin. It can puff up its beard to look scarier to attackers.

Central bearded dragons are omnivores, which means they eat meat and plants. They have a strong bite and a sticky tongue that helps them catch their prey. They are good climbers and have been found sitting on fence posts and tree branches.

GREEN
ANACONDA

Green anacondas live in swamps, marshes and slow-moving waters in South America. They are good swimmers and often hunt in water. They can open their mouths really wide to swallow prey whole. They can survive without eating for weeks or even months after a big meal.

Green anacondas are constrictors. This means they kill their prey by wrapping their strong bodies around it and squeezing tight. The prey dies because it cannot breathe.

KOMODO DRAGON

Komodo dragons live in Indonesia and are the largest lizards in the world. They will eat whatever prey they can find. They eat carrion (dead animals) but also hunt large animals such as deer and water buffalo.

Komodo dragons wait for prey to come close to them before attacking with their sharp teeth and claws. If prey gets away, Komodo dragons will follow it until it dies, then eat it.

RETICULATED
PYTHON

Reticulated pythons are the longest snakes in the world. They live in warm forests in Southeast Asia and are good at climbing trees. They are also good swimmers and can often be found in or near water.

Reticulated pythons are
constrictors. They eat
mammals such as large deer
or pigs. They can sense heat,
which helps them find prey
hiding in leaves or in the dark.

NILE
CROCODILE

Adult Nile crocodiles are apex predators. This means they do not have any predators themselves. Nile crocodiles are known to eat whatever prey they can find. Baby Nile crocodiles eat small prey, such as insects.

Nile crocodiles eat spiky porcupines, small hippos, and zebras. They can eat prey as large as wildebeest. They also eat carrion and have been known to attack humans that get too close to them.

WEIGHT A MINUTE

Congratulations, you met the predators. They are all very fierce and some of them are very heavy, too. Let's see how much these reptiles can weigh. Komodo dragons weigh around 135 kilograms and alligator snapping turtles weigh up to 100 kilograms.

Nile crocodiles are very heavy – they weigh up to 900 kilograms. Green anacondas weigh around 227 kilograms, but king cobras only weigh around 9 kilograms.

QUESTIONS

1: **Where does a Gila monster store fat?**
a) In its eyes
b) In its tail
c) Under a big rock

2: **What does carrion mean?**

3: **What is the longest venomous snake in the world?**

4: **How does the alligator snapping turtle catch prey?**

5: **Which predator do you think is the scariest?**